Imagined Sons

in memory of my beloved mother,
Bernadine Meeker Etter (1945-2011),

and for my son

Imagined Sons

Carrie Etter

SEREN

Seren is the book imprint of
Poetry Wales Press Ltd.
57 Nolton Street, Bridgend, Wales, CF31 3AE
www.serenbooks.com
facebook.com/SerenBooks
Twitter:@SerenBooks

The right of Carrie Etter to be identified as
the author of this work has been asserted in accordance
with the Copyright, Designs and Patents Act, 1988.

ISBN: 978-1-78172-151-3
ISBN:e-book: 978-1-78172-154-4
Mobi/Kindle ISBN: 978-1-78172-155-1

A CIP record for this title is available from the British Library.

The publisher acknowledges the financial assistance of the Welsh Books Council.

Cover Image: 'St. Christina' by Paula Rego, 2009. By kind permission of the artist.

Printed in Bembo by Bell & Bain Ltd. Glasgow.

Author's Website: http://carrieetter.blogspot.co.uk/

Contents

'Do not forget your moon is my moon & that each
  morning I remember

You by the distance I have put between us.'

> – Sophie Cabot Black, 'The Arguments'

'It seems courage is lack of alternatives.'

> – Deborah Digges, 'The New World'

A Birthmother's Catechism

How did you let him go?

With black ink and legalese

How did you let him go?

It'd be another year before I could vote

How did you let him go?

With altruism, tears and self-loathing

How did you let him go?

A nurse brought pills for drying up breast milk

How did you let him go?

Who hangs a birdhouse from a sapling?

Imagined Sons 1: Fairy Tale

My son leans from the tower; his red pompadour, stiff with Aqua Net, resists the quick wind. When he sings, the notes hasten to the forest a mile south before they descend. I clamber onto my restless horse; she starts before I am secure. Almost too soon we reach the wood.

The notes are red. I pluck them like poppies.

Imagined Sons 2: Delivery

Pushing a trolley stacked with grocery crates, a delivery man follows me on the circuitous route to my flat. 'I'm surprised you found it so easily,' I say, 'your first time.'

'I've been here before,' he replies.

'So you know Bradford on Avon?' I say, walking slowly up the slope.

'No,' he says, out of breath, as though the incline's steeper, as though he's Sisyphus, 'I know *you*.'

Imagined Sons 3: Seed Corn

Illinois

I hear his hands moving through the dry cornstalks, cracking off ears and tossing them in a barrow. The hard grains will serve as next year's seed: this is the crop that yields the next. I run my fingers along the dead stalks as I go, making the field whisper and crackle, occasionally cutting a fingertip on the husks' sharp lines.

I am far enough away that he reckons me the wind when he hears the susurrus of my passing. Only as he approaches the field's edge, nearing the house, does he begin to suspect a human presence, once lost and now, possibly, retrievable. That's what he senses as he increases his pace and at last breaks into a run, always gaining on a memory he can't quite catch.

Imagined Sons 4: Black and Velvet

I see a group of teenage goths outside Fopp, and one girl's mélange of black chiffon and crimson velvet reminds me of a previous self. I look at the boy she leans against, with studs in his nose, eyebrow and chin, and silver, inch-wide hoops inside his lobes, and I look away, feeling queasy.

But as I turn, our eyes meet, and his flashing glare says he saw an unintended look of revulsion. And it occurs to me, as I head into the shop, that he is about my height, that he has my large, dark eyes, and that to glance back would evoke a sneer.

I remember The Sisters of Mercy, a band I listened to in those black and velvet days, and start browsing my way toward them from the beginning of the alphabet, thinking to avoid him, thinking to meet.

Imagined Sons 5: Reunion

Normal, Illinois

I walk into my old high school and run a hand over the lockers as I try to remember which was mine. Turning a corner, I see a classmate, Mark, somehow appearing just as he did at seventeen. As I approach, he mutters, 'Slut,' and stepping into the stairwell I see a gauntlet of old classmates lined up to greet me thus. I hurry down, cringing, and see one face I don't recognise at first.

It's you, grown to the age I was when I gave you up. Your hands clench, your face flushes as you chant, louder than the others, *'Whore, whore, whore.'*

A Birthmother's Catechism (September 11, 1986)

What is the anniversary of loss?

A national day of mourning

Really now, what is the anniversary of loss?

My mother and I watch TV well past her usual bedtime

What is the anniversary of loss?

Where the swan's nest had been, widely scattered branches and some crumpled beer cans

What is the anniversary of loss?

Sometimes the melancholy arrives before the remembering

What is the anniversary of loss?

Some believe it is impossible to spend too much on the memorial

What is the anniversary of loss?

When I say sometimes the melancholy comes first, I know the body has its own memory

What is the anniversary of loss?

The wishbone snapped, and I clung to the smaller piece

Imagined Sons 6: Introducing Myself As His (The First Supermarket Dream)

His hand strikes my cheek, and I shudder and sting. His eyes tear and close, his mouth sucks in his lips. The okra and the mangoes are watching; the stock boy and the trio of cheerleaders consider plots. Reflexively I reach toward him, but what reflex is this, so long unused? 'My mother is at home,' he stammers as he recoils. 'I'm sorry.'

'I'm sorry,' I whisper to the yams. 'Yes, your mother is at home.'

Imagined Sons 7: *The Big Issue*

London

As I climb the steps to Hungerford Bridge, I feel in my pocket for change – I'll be asked to buy *The Big Issue* before I reach the other side.

A blind man could discriminate between the Londoners and the tourists: the former hurry on as the latter loiter and stare. I weave my way at a leisurely pace.

I see a scruffy boy of a man selling and approach him. 'Two-fifty, isn't it?' I say, and he nods while extending a hand for my coins.

'Thank you, ma'am,' he says, and I'm surprised to hear a familiar accent.

I tilt my head, trying to see around his long fringe, to see his eyes. 'You're American, too,' I say, shoving the magazine in my bag. 'Where are you from?'

Imagined Sons 8: The Businessman

My son gazes from the skyscraper's twenty-third floor, his waxy hair set in rigorous waves. When he sighs, he checks to see if anyone hears him, but does not think to look below. Downward the sigh drifts like first snow, to melt at the touch, so I stand with my head thrown back and my mouth open, to catch it if I can.

Imagined Sons 9: Greek Salad

For a week I travel on business, and on the fourth afternoon, I go to a restaurant to have yet another meal alone. I order a Greek salad and read a Dickens novel to escape my loneliness.

When the salad arrives, I barely look. How will Jenny Wren respond to news of her drunken father's death? I push the fork into the lettuce, and it yields slowly to the tines. The balance of balsamic vinegar and olive oil, with the sweetness of the red lettuce, is perfect, and I pause, relishing the flavour.

I hear the smallest of shrieks. I think I must have anticipated Jenny, that I must have been that engrossed, when I hear it again. I put my book down so its open pages press the plastic tablecloth and keep my place, and my fork dives again, spearing a cube of feta.

'Stop! Stop!' The sound rises from the salad.

'Who – what are you?' I whisper. '*Where* are you?'

A black olive wiggles atop a romaine leaf, as though to wave. 'I am your son, brutally transformed!'

I glance around the restaurant and see the other diners, all in groups, engaged in conversation. 'When I last saw you, you were an infant. How did you get into this state?' I say with some sharpness.

I think I see him cringe. Meekly, he says, 'I fell in love with the virgin mistress of the god's own olive grove. When I made love to her, I was turned into an olive tree!'

'When you made love to her?'

The softest of whispers: '*They* say, when I raped her.'

'So you are a tree as well as this olive?' I ask, trying to move my mouth as little as possible as I see the waiter coming from the kitchen. 'So she tends to you, there in the grove?'

'She only knows I disappeared,' the olive whines. 'She tends to me, yes, but without thought, without love. It is a fate worse than –'

'Delicious,' I say to the waiter, swallowing the small olive whole. 'Just delicious.'

A Birthmother's Catechism

Who do you think you are?

A musical phrase remembered from time to time for no apparent reason

Who do you think you are?

A wrong answer

Who do you think you are?

An aptitude for words his parents do not share

Who do you think you are?

The vestige of an unacknowledged longing

Who do you think you are?

Eve

Who do you think you are?

No one, no one at all

Imagined Sons 10: Mexico

I wake fifty yards from the shore of Baja California, in a remote campground near San Quintin. I lie listening to the waves until the tent's stale air urges me out.

Dunes slope into the distance, and from my last visit I know that as I walk beside them I'll find sand dollars. I want to take some away perfect for my nieces and nephews, but one I have to break open, to see once again five immaculately sculpted, tiny white doves.

After breakfast, I begin my walk. A few minutes along, I see an impression of a sand dollar, where one must have been since the last high tide. After a few more steps, I find another such outline and start to think someone else has recently come with the same motive.

At the sixth impression, I see a figure in the distance. No matter how I increase my pace, the figure remains shadowy, no larger, no smaller, always taking the crisp, white discs, leaving me nothing over and over again.

Imagined Sons 11: The Friend (Part 1)

At the park, I find the bench and watch families, couples and solitary dog-walkers stroll by. After a while, a young man, tall and thin with wispy blonde hair, sits down at the other end of the bench.

'You're not him,' I say, suppressing a sigh.

'No, but I'm his friend. I've come to take you to him.'

I jump to my feet, and he rises to my side.

After a few minutes, I ask, 'Is he close?,' walking so quickly I nearly run.

'Yes, just ahead,' he replies, not meeting my gaze.

We pass through a stand of trees, sunlight sprinkling the path as the canopy of leaves shifts, rustling, with breezes. Coming out on the other side, I'm surprised to see no people, no one visible in the distance, only low stones, tablets of grey and black, occasionally a white cross, and I apprehend that this is a —

Imagined Sons 12: The Birthmother,
The Adoptive Mother & Their Surfer Boy

Venice Beach, California

Never falling, he rides the wave. I've been here for years. Long ago, a tall woman in a cream-coloured suit sat near me on the sand. I asked her to watch my towel and nectarines while I hurried to the bathroom; on my return, I saw juice on her chin. Weeks later, I confided, 'That's my son,' pointing as he glided toward us on a six-foot wave. 'He's *mine*,' she snapped. She pulled off my pointing arm as easily as if it were a mannequin's and cast it into the water, before running into the ocean and swimming toward him. Knocking his surfboard aside, she slid under his feet and floated to the surface: hair the dark red of a nectarine pit, lips fixed in a victorious smirk. All the while my arm drifts slowly, surely toward him – and toward her.

Imagined Sons 13: The Woodcutter

Kenai, Alaska

I stand in his line of vision, but he continues to split logs in one
or two swings of the ax. I leave, and when I return an hour later,
I set my stump ten feet from his and drop an armload of wood
alongside it. Trying to hew my first piece, I knock the edge, and
off the log spins. On the second try, I cut away a switch of bark.
When I replace the log for a third attempt, his hands are on
mine, showing me how to grip the handle, how to hold my
arms, how, in an afternoon, to cut enough wood to warm us
both.

A Birthmother's Catechism

What is the holiday of loss?

Mother's Day

What is the holiday of loss?

Celebrate your mother with three courses for 19.95

What is the holiday of loss?

A pot of forget-me-nots tied with pink ribbon

What is the holiday of loss?

Two bottles of good wine

What is the holiday of loss?

No one, not even the rain, had such small hands

Imagined Sons 14: Five Star

As the cab pulls up at my hotel, the door to my left opens, and before I step out, the doorman draws my suitcase from the trunk. 'Welcome to New York,' he says warmly, and gesturing to the building's height, adds, 'This is all yours – how do you like that?' I laugh and smile as he guides me through the revolving door into the lobby, as he remarks on the differing character of the two interior bars and sweeps me up to reception. I've hardly thanked and tipped him when he whisks back to the entrance, to greet the next arrival. It's just as I expected: he has no more time for me than anyone else.

Imagined Sons 15: The Second Supermarket Dream

When I reach the cashier, I'm already five minutes late for my appointment. I rummage through the bottom of my purse for more change. 'Sorry,' I say. 'Just give me a minute.'

'Take all the time you want. You're my last customer.'

Coins collected, I meet his gaze and shudder. He's reasonably handsome, with his father's reddish hair and light eyes.

'Mango and okra – what are you making?' he says, bemused, holding out his hand.

The silver splatters back into my purse. I extend my fingers and feel the warmth of his own before the face pales, the eyes darken, and I see a stranger, pimpled and cringing: 'Lady?'

Imagined Sons 16: Narcissus

I see first his reflection in the pond, a fainter version of his silken face. When I sit on the grass beside him and say, 'I've come at last,' the echo reproaches me, *at last at last at last*, and he, undisturbed, continues to admire himself. I try again with, 'I'm so glad to see you,' but the echo hisses with accusation, *you you you*. I break into sobs, and when the water of my tears laps at my feet, I know I'm here to drown us both.

Imagined Sons 17: The Courthouse

I sit in the last row. When I read the notice in the paper six weeks ago, I thought about taking up knitting, so I could busy my hands and eyes as needed. Instead I have become nondescript, the murky darkness of dishwater.

You arrive in a cheap suit and handcuffs. I am the surprise witness, an unforeseen alibi, another story about who you are and how you got here. Your father will swear me in.

A Birthmother's Catechism

Why haven't you looked for him?

I could paper these walls with rejection slips

Why haven't you looked for him?

When he was fourteen, I moved to England

Why haven't you looked for him?

I just need to pick up some milk

Why haven't you looked for him?

There's a blissful patience on the Hanged Man's face

Why haven't you looked for him?

My office is rarely tidy

Why haven't you looked for him?

I expected my parents to live longer

Why haven't you looked for him?

For the rain it raineth every day

Why haven't you looked for him?

What if I found him?

Why haven't you looked for him?

What if I found him turning away?

Imagined Sons 18: Used Cars

I enter the lot and approach a blue car. Beaming a toothy smile, a young man in a shiny silver suit begins twisting his way toward me.

He likes to talk, so I let him. Every so often I nod or ask a question, and that keeps him running for at least another five minutes.

In less than an hour though we're at the other end of the lot, only one blue car left, and he wants me to 'give it a go'.

How can I tell him I don't drive?

Imagined Sons 19: The Baker

Bradford on Avon, England

The chime jingles as I close the door behind me and am about to say, 'Sliced granary today, Stuart,' but it is not the ever-contented Stuart standing behind the counter. Some younger, paler man has taken his place, and behind him are not the usual shelves of various breads, pastries and baps. Every loaf is sliced granary, what I'd thought, moments before, would suit the sandwiches for today's long walk. Already the young man holds forth a loaf, his awkward posture betraying some uneasiness as he says, 'This is it, right? This is what you wanted?'

Imagined Sons 20: The Friend (Part 2)

He holds before him a takeout tub. 'Pad see-eew, with chicken,' he says. A white fork lies on top of the container, and without speaking, I take the utensil with one hand, the tub with the other.

I've been sleeping on the grave for the past four? six? nights. In the day I hide in the grove. There is nothing to say to my son's friend, who comes and goes with reassuring tenacity.

I sit down, cross-legged, and begin to eat. I can't conceive how he knows about pad see-eew or steak fajitas or kung pao scallops, but he does; each time he arrives with food and drink and stories.

And I stay because I cannot leave. And I stay to listen when the cicadas grow cacophonous and his voice, allied with but not, not *his*, is all that I hear.

Imagined Sons 21: The Friend (Part 3)

His friend brings me a shoelace, twelve photos, two unposted letters, a worry stone, a restaurant receipt and a brown leather bomber jacket. At night I alternate between using the jacket as a pillow and as a blanket. Either way I wake to a span of years carved into grey stone – thousands, thousands of irreclaimable days.

A Birthmother's Catechism

What do you remember?

Thick fingers knead and knead an emptied womb

What do you remember?

A pair of arms a weighted cradle

What do you remember?

'No One Is to Blame' on the radio all summer

What do you remember?

The nurse ignored the gown's two wet circles and brought a bottle at feeding time

What do you remember?

A rocking chair in an unlit room

What do you remember?

Everything, but the drive away

Imagined Sons 22: Prague

I stand on the cobbled stones with a hundred other tourists, all looking up, some readying cameras, as we wait for the astronomical clock to strike.

On the hour, the procession of the twelve apostles across its face begins. The wooden figures jerk one way then another as they move on a mechanism invisible from here.

Under the sound of the bell, there's a frenzy of clicks, beeps and whirrs as the cameras go, and a flash stuns me. *Somebody's got theirs turned the wrong way round,* I assume as I blink away negatives, until I notice a young man running away.

Imagined Sons 23: Blood

I arrive at the health centre for my blood test. The teenage girl scheduled before me stealthily nibbles at her nails.

The nurse is a young man who stammers as he calls the girl's name. I look away, and once the door is closed, their voices rise and fall as he speaks more loudly and her volume increases in unison before he shushes her and they speak in hushed voices once again. After a few minutes she emerges with shining eyes.

I think of his potentially unsteady hands and contemplate leaving, but before I can decide, he appears in the door frame and announces my name. Just looking at me seems to calm him, renewing the routine: a stranger, a briefly disturbing stranger as he considers and dismisses a feeling of recognition, and so a stranger once again.

Imagined Sons 24: The Lone Star State

The La Quinta Inn near the capitol looks, at first glance, like a stucco Escher, pink walkways and stairwells in endless concatenation. Approaching the counter, I find the attendant's supple skin and rising brows all the more youthful for their incongruity with the building. Or perhaps that immaturity, the nascent masculinity that has altered his voice but failed to give him stubble, provides the ballast, the element necessary for such elaborate infrastructure to cohere.

'I'm afraid there's no record of your reservation,' he says, looking at a monitor. 'But I've got a sofa bed at home, and a six-pack of Negra Modelo in the fridge – there's so much catching up to do.'

'And that *is* my favourite beer,' I reply lightly, gingerly, grasping the handle of my suitcase.

He leads me out of the lobby, along a walkway, and up a flight of stairs, his step quickening. When he turns a corner, eluding my gaze, I call the name I gave him nineteen years ago and try to revive the image of his ID badge. I hear his steps but cannot catch up, so I hurry after, calling along the corridors, through the stairwells, past ice machines, housekeeping, the swimming pool, with my suitcase always rolling behind me, until at last I see the lobby and rush through the automatic doors to the desk.

He looks up, bewildered and innocent. 'Welcome to La Quinta, ma'am. May I help you?'

Imagined Sons 25: The Train Home

I feel a touch, then a shake, a grip of my shoulder. I open my eyes, and the young man snatches his hand back. 'You're getting off at Bath, right?' he asks. I straighten up, struggling to wake. 'We're almost there.'

'Oh, thanks,' I manage and look out the window. I see the high stone walls that indicate we're just a minute or so out.

I rub my eyes and slowly gather my bags. The train pulls into the station, and I rise, wondering how the man knew my stop, knew me. I glance about and see he's just a few steps away. He's not much taller than I am, and his eyes are as large and dark as my own.

He smiles, coming closer. 'This is my stop, too.'

A Birthmother's Catechism

Where have you been?

Pressed against the nursery glass

Where have you been?

I slept the sleep of the dead

Where have you been?

Normal's midway between St. Louis and Chicago

Where have you been?

My four sisters have twelve children among them

Where have you been?

Right here, at the hospital entrance, as though waiting
for a swallow

Imagined Sons 26: The Third Supermarket Dream

He has come between work and dinner, when carts clang into one another coming round corners and tight smiles suppress curses. I slide past him, first speaking to a stock boy, later making small talk with a trio of cheerleaders in matching sweaters and short, pleated skirts. When his gaze turns in my direction, I wander away, unable to leave with my okra and mango, and unable to be found, and found wanting.

Imagined Sons 27: The Fourth Supermarket Dream

'It's *your* birthday,' I say. 'What do *you* want for dinner?'

He grins. 'How about ribs?'

I swing the cart toward the meat coolers, and he keeps pace at my side.

The items in the cart rise: barbecue sauce, sour cream, an angel food cake, potatoes, two cobs of corn, chives, salted butter, a box of candles, white frosting, a six-pack of Negra Modelo....

Who knows if we will ever leave?

Imagined Sons 28: The Pilot

Two hours into the Bristol-Newark flight, the seatbelt symbol lights up with a loud ding: turbulence. Moments after, a young man, barely of age, emerges from the cockpit in a navy suit and matching cap. Coming down the aisle, humming, he surveys the rows to either side with a proprietary air as he passes. Passengers whisper to one another and point, and a squeal rises when the plane jolts, but his placid expression doesn't acknowledge it.

At my row he halts and asks with a smile, 'How ya doin', ma'am?'

I glance about, noting quizzical looks. 'I – I'm fine. Are you – the pilot?' I hear the woman next to me swallow hard as I say it.

His grin broadens. 'That would be worrying, wouldn't it? Your life in someone else's hands, someone not really grown up yet, you not able to do anything about it....'

Softly I respond, 'You're not the pilot. You're too young to be the pilot.'

The plane shudders, and he turns, running back the way he came, becoming younger with each stride until he falls into the arms of a scowling woman, into the shape of an infant, swaddled in navy blue.

Imagined Sons 29: The Friend (Part 4)

'It's time to go,' his friend says, and I sigh and nod. He heads to the grove to collect my things.

I wait and wonder what's taking him when I realise he's staying away deliberately. I smooth my hand along the top of the head-stone, as though smoothing my son's hair; I press my lips to each letter of his name and murmur, alternating, *Hello, Good-bye, Hello, Good-bye.* When, after the last letter, I say, *Hello,* I gasp and twist my hands, but then I breathe and repeat, *Hello hello hello hello hello....*

A Birthmother's Catechism

What do you want?

After twenty hours on trains, I stand on the platform and
stare at I know not what

What do you want?

Rub the leaves between your fingers and smell a ripe lemon

What do you want?

When a stranger compares her mortgage to signing away
her firstborn, I nod and cannot speak

What do you want?

The hangman sold the rope by the inch as a panacea

What do you want?

Houndstooth daisies, in a small, extended fist

Imagined Sons 30: Drury Lane, London

Between appointments, I pop into Oxfam on Drury Lane and browse through clothes; I pass over the pastels to the earth tones and linger there. I see a rich chocolate cardigan and reach for it.

'Oh, I'm sorry,' an American girl says as her hand brushes mine – she'd gone for the same sweater. 'You go ahead.'

'Thanks,' I reply, drawing down the hanger and tucking it under my arm. She's found a maroon blouse that looks just my style, and I give her a better look, this American teenager whose taste overlaps with mine. She has a slight figure and wears a lot of makeup – powdery, pinked cheeks, light mascara, shimmering eyelids – and her heels are a height I haven't dared in years.

And I notice, in a small patch along the jaw, a place where the foundation and powder have faded or been inadvertently rubbed off – revealing the faintest shadow of stubble.

I turn back to the rack, losing myself in the greens, when again I hear that voice and sense what she is working up the nerve to say.

Imagined Sons 31: Folk Night at The George

The room is lit with white candles in wine bottles. Around the perimeter sit thirty-some people, with handwritten songs, accordions, guitars and two fiddles. I see an open seat on a far bench and return nods of recognition and perhaps gratitude (for who else comes only to listen?) as I make my way around small tables and over instrument cases. Soon the music begins.

After half an hour, we come to a long-haired young man with a guitar. He plays and sings a kind of sea shanty, but rather than the sailing husband lost in the waves, the man asks the water where his mother has gone. I lean towards Jack on my right and whisper, 'Do you know this song?', and he shakes his head and shrugs.

In the applause that follows, Jack asks, 'I don't know that one. Where'd you get it from?'

The young man replies, 'I wrote it. I mean, it's based on traditional shanties, but I made the arrangement and wrote the lyrics.'

'Really?' I say, leaning forward. 'What gave you the idea?'

Imagined Sons 32: The Fifth Supermarket Dream

I lower a jar of salsa into the cart and am startled, on rising, to face a panting young man. He looks about, and when a fifty-some woman in a lavender suit appears at the end of the aisle, he pleads in a whisper, 'Get me out of here. I can't have her catch me again.'

I am about to say yes when a manicured hand firmly clasps my shoulder. It is the same woman — indeed there are at least a dozen of them — all with tightly bound dark hair, all closing and sure to bear him away, when I start swinging with impeccable aim.

Imagined Sons 33: Franklin Park

Bloomington, Illinois

The day after my mother's funeral, I find an obscure, level spot and brush it free of twigs; and I lie down in that space as though it were my grave. I close my eyes.

After a few minutes, I hear, at the other end of this large square of a park, a crunching footfall. Then the crackle rises and falls in sweeps, and after a while I grasp that someone is gathering leaves into a high, fragile mound.

Now a voice, a young man's voice, in a whoop of delight as he runs crashing into the heap, as he falls into breaking noise. A moment later he is rustling, reassembling the pile, and this time he walks farther away, takes a longer run-up to the shout and spill.

After he leaves, I rise to my feet and take the shorter route home.

A Birthmother's Catechism (September 11, 2006)

What day is today?

The sorrows have been catalogued

What day is today?

We observed minutes of silence for the lost

What day is today?

His twentieth birthday: old enough to vote, too young to drink

What day is today?

The Stars and Stripes hang half-mast

What day is today?

In the full glare of the son —

What day is today?

I take a table in the sun and find it too bright to see

Imagined Sons 34: Lemonade

McLean County, Illinois

On an empty summer afternoon, I head into the prairie on an old bicycle. I race on dusty tarmac, the air thick with the smell of green, cornstalks at full height, their husks brimming.

The field gives way to a farmstead, where I see a card table with the sign LEMON AID 25¢. There's a boy, about ten, sitting in a lawn chair until he jumps to attention.

I pull up and dig in a pocket for change. 'I'll take a glass,' I say, and slowly pouring he fills a small cup. I lay a quarter on the table and push it towards him.

I'm swallowing the cup in one when he speaks to me for the first time: 'We thought you'd never get here.' I choke on my drink, sputtering, and see in the distance a young man in t-shirt and jeans, hands in his pockets, but his expression is indiscernible from so far away.

I wipe the back of my hand across my wet lips and onto my thigh. I draw out two more quarters and extend my hand. 'Then I'm going to need some more.'

Imagined Sons 35: Enoteca de Belem, Lisbon

Down a side street, on the right, lies Enoteca, respite from the deep heat and crowds of tourists. I take Trevor's hand to lead him inside.

Late afternoon, there is only a handful of customers. I head for my favourite table, furthest from the street. We sit as the sommelier flourishes menus.

He sets down two glasses of water and smiles. 'Miss, you are from Illinois, am I right?'

'Yessss,' I say in two syllables, as I wonder where he's headed. 'I am.'

He gestures to the back of a man at the bar. 'This young man, he too is from Illinois.'

'Is that right?' I say as the man turns to us and nods. I raise my brows, waiting.

A few seconds pass before my fellow Illinoisan looks at me and says, 'I heard you like your wine.'

Imagined Sons 36: The Bus

When I get on the bus to go to work, the driver winks at me. Winks! I take my ticket and choose a seat; there's only one other passenger, and he rides in the very back. The wink has jostled me into curiosity, and when it occurs to me that yes, the driver's features seem vaguely familiar, I realise that the other passenger is coming closer. I look over my shoulder and see him, dark-haired with downcast eyes, advance a row. When I look into the driver's rearview mirror, I am surprised to see reflected two casts of the same face, not twins but somehow the same person twice over, driven and driver, my son and my son, as the bus takes a turn away from its route, past a field greener than any I have ever seen.

Imagined Sons 37: Night Patrols

After three rapes in four weeks, the night patrols reach an all-time high, and *The Bath Chronicle* reports each infinitesimal development in all caps. I begin avoiding the narrow passageways I normally prefer, but one night, after drinks, I forget, instinctively following an old route, until a hand grabs my shoulder.

I pull away with a jerk, but he's got my elbow, now my upper arm, and when we face, we halt in mutual recognition. His jaw drops, but he does not or cannot let go, so I draw back my free arm and strike – I hit him as hard as I can.

Imagined Sons 38: DJ

All right y'all driving home from work tonight, you've had a hard day and now we've got some songs to help you forget — but first, you'll forgive a man on his birthday one song for remembering. This goes out to, well, I don't know her name, but I'll say I was born in Peoria, Illinois, twenty years ago today. Here's Joni Mitchell, her music all done when she found her daughter, but such a legacy — here's 'Little Green' for you, you know who you are.

A Birthmother's Catechism

When will you let him go?

A man carves my name into granite with hammer and chisel

When will you let him go?

My grandmother's hair was never white

When will you let him go?

This door cannot be lifted off its hinges

When will you let him go?

Take two of my ribs to make a fire

When will you let him go?

It is time, Celan said, the stone made an effort to flower

Acknowledgements

Grateful acknowledgment is made to the editors of the follow-ing publications, in which many of these poems have appeared: *Ambit, Barrow Street, The Iowa Review, Long Poem Magazine, New Walk, New Welsh Review, PN Review, The Republic of Letters* and *The Times Literary Supplement.* Some of these poems were also published in a pamphlet, *The Son* (Oystercatcher, 2009), which was the Poetry Book Society's Pamphlet Choice for Autumn 2009.

I am also happy to acknowledge the generosity of the Society of Authors, who awarded me an Authors' Foundation grant toward the completion of this book.

The quote from Celan on page 57 is from 'Corona' from *Poems of Paul Celan*, translated by Michael Hamburger, Anvil, 2007.

Thanks to Moniza Alvi, Matt Bryden, Claire Crowther and Ian Duhig for their considered reading of various versions of the manuscript and their tremendous encouragement. For generos-ity of spirit, I must also thank Simon Avery, Lynn Corr, Francesca Francoli, Tony Frazer, Trevor Lillistone, Rachel McCarthy, Susan Mackervoy, Jennifer Militello, Bernard O'Donoghue, Molly Peacock, Hilda Sheehan, Mimi Thebo and my editor, Amy Wack.

Likewise I am grateful to my family, friends and students whose support continues to sustain me. Thanks to you all.

About the Author

After growing up in Normal, Illinois, Carrie Etter lived in southern California for thirteen years before moving to England in 2001. A poet, fiction writer and critic, she has published two collections, *The Tethers* (Seren, 2009), winner of the London New Poetry Prize, and *Divining for Starters* (Shearsman, 2011); she also edited *Infinite Difference: Other Poetries by UK Women Poets* (Shearsman, 2010). Her reviews have appeared in *The Guardian, The Independent, Poetry Review* and *Verse*, among others, and she keeps a blog at http://carrieetter.blogspot.com. Since 2004 she has been a member of the creative writing faculty at Bath Spa University.